# Skinny Dipping with Loons

## Uncommon Stories of the Everyday

LAURIE CASWELL BURKE

Published by Wind Ridge Publishing, Inc.
P.O. Box 752
Shelburne, Vermont 05482

ISBN Number:  978-1-935922-02-5
Library of Congress PCN: 2010941233

Book and cover design by Laurie Thomas
Printed in Burlington, Vermont, U.S.A.

# Skinny Dipping with Loons

## Uncommon Stories of the Everyday

## LAURIE CASWELL BURKE

Published by Wind Ridge Publishing, Inc.
Shelburne, Vermont

# Contents

"To be a person is to have a story to tell."

—*Karen Blixen/Isak Dineson*

In loving memory of my father, Henry Wright Caswell, who inspired my writing and to my daughters, Molly and Kate, whom I hope to inspire.

# Gratitude

*T*hese stories evolved out of a desire to capture and give voice to certain parts of my life that have meaning: the places, people, and adventures that have shaped me. Perhaps, much like my personality, I let these tales flow from memory without too much interference, or particular logic and sequence. However, it is difficult to put together a collection of stories like this without support. I am indeed grateful for the abundant guidance and help I received on many fronts. I would like to express my deepest gratitude to several special people.

First, thank you to Holly Bartlett Johnson and her capable team at Wind Ridge Publishing for making this possible through their amazing generosity. And to Lin Stone who is the sweetest, kindest editor you could ever imagine and is filled with infinite "pearls of wisdom" to inform your process. As I moved along I felt Lin's voice sitting with me reminding me to add details, such as the "wren in the sycamore" rather than the "bird in the tree." Thank you also to Laurie Thomas for her help with book's design and production.

I am also grateful to my very first fiction writing teacher, Philip Baruth, who spent many hours reading my stories and offered brilliant advice. Additionally, he upheld my confidence that I could succeed at this endeavor. Above all, his inspiration helped me to frame my stories from the place called Humpty – a place that always feeds my heart and soul, and a place where many folks who may read this book will have shared time and memories.

Thank you to my close friends, Heidi Bock, Sue Dixon,

Charlotte Albers, Hilary Maslow, Susan Bouchard, Lisa Desmond, Melinda Walsh, and Ann Schroeder who listened patiently to some of my readings during this process. In particular, thank you to my friend Jennifer Francoeur who endured countless readings and provided thoughtful and heartfelt feedback.

Last but not least, thank you to my family: thank you to my sister Annie, the talented artist who illustrated this book; to my proud mom, Sally Caswell, for her faith in me; to my husband Tim, and my daughters, Kate and Molly, for their patience.

When the writing was completed, I realized that I had unintentionally covered many aspects of my life, ranging from my younger years, through to college and young adult years, to today, when I find myself traversing middle age.

I know that hospice workers and others say that, as people get closer to the end of their lives, they want and perhaps need to tell their life stories. But I say, why wait? I hope to inspire everyone to make the time to do this now, and not later. It's fun to revisit the times and adventures of younger years and to conjure up the emotions that were a part of it all. It is amazing that so much returns to you when you allow yourself the time to remember. Whether it was my recollection of my grandmother's fur coat and the scent of her Joy perfume during boring church sermons, or the moment I saw my parents' car nosedive into the pond, I was amazed at the power of recall.

I have learned from observing others that we can achieve our dreams if we have focus and are willing to work hard. I also know the value of following your passions. I have always dreamed of writing a book, and now here it is, held in my hand and in yours too, just waiting to be read. I hope you enjoy the stories as much as I have enjoyed writing them, and perhaps in one or two you will find something that rings true and familiar. But most of all, I hope that these stories may inspire you to remember to share and tell your stories too.

# Humpty

*W*e are fortunate if we have a special place where we can go and feel completely at home. For me, that place is called Humpty. It is a cabin that rests beside a running brook that is nestled in Vermont's Green Mountains with a view of Camel's Hump, hence the cabin's name. My father built it on a large parcel of land he bought in the sixties. He wanted this parcel of land so much that he drove seven hours from our suburban Vermont home to New Jersey in a blinding snowstorm on my brother's seventh birthday to sign the purchase papers.

Originally, my dad built a rustic cabin complete with a pot-bellied stove for heat and a makeshift sink. The deck was constructed from repurposed old football bleachers. Years later, he constructed a more substantial structure with a barnboard interior, wagon wheel lights, and a winding staircase leading to the loft. The fireplace was built with stones from the property and one stone that was stuck smack in the center read 1867. The cabin was stable and sound, and held a comforting feeling when you stepped inside.

Our cabin once overlooked a peaceful valley and from the front porch there was a perfect view of Camel's Hump. Over time, the trees have hidden our beloved view of the mountain and valley, reminders that perspectives, as well as life, always change. My father passed on during his mid-life years, and Humpty was his legacy to our family.

Almost fifty years later, Humpty has grown to almost legendary status. Over the years, we have shared Humpty's peace and beauty with friends and family for countless special occasions and family gatherings. It has provided the backdrop for many fond and funny memories; if Humpty's walls could talk it would fill volumes. Among my favorite stories are the memories of my parents' car nose-diving into the pond, bare bottoms in the 1970s streaking around the cabin, and myriad matchmaking schemes. Many of the wilder stories involved Humpty's wildlife. On more than one occasion, we've chased flying squirrels out of the house armed with flashlights and brooms, we've reluctantly shared living space with squatting families of mice and cluster flies. Once we withstood a break-in and entry by a scoundrel raccoon that almost destroyed our cabin's furnishings. For many years, families of snakes made their home in a cutlery drawer next to the kitchen sink. It's true. We would quickly get rid of them only to find that they always found their way back. Visitors to our mountain abode often warily asked about the infamous snake drawer.

Another of my favorite Humpty stories took place at my oldest daughter Molly's sixth birthday party. That particular year the party's theme was nature and included a scavenger hunt and assorted nature-themed games. Cups, plates, and tablecloths all donned a wildlife motif. When it came time for cake, decorated with colorful birds, ladybugs, and butterflies, I asked one of the mothers to retrieve a knife from the cutlery drawer, overlooking any potential hazards or unwelcome surprises assuming that the snakes had long since departed. When the screams began, I became concerned. The only word I could make out was "Snakes." Moments later the young mother came out screaming,

"Snakes…snakes… snakes in the drawer." Behind her was a fifteen-year-old boy, the son of one of my friends, carrying a butterfly net filled with five or six snakes. Screams and squeals accompanied children and parents exiting the porch, as the candles melted into the cake. Our birthday celebration was transformed into a wild scene in just moments. Our fifteen-year-old boy hopped off the porch with a Cheshire cat grin, butterfly net, snakes in tow, and delivered the snake family to a more suitable abode.

In time, we found a way to permanently block the hole that allowed the slimy long creatures to slither in for warmth. We also moved the cutlery to a new location. Once things had settled that day, I confess there was a little bit of satisfaction in knowing that the impromptu incident topped off a nature-themed children's party perfectly.

# Spring Fling

*I*t started out like many Friday afternoons. The usual gang gathered at the library steps, books and backpacks in hand to catch the afternoon sun as we collectively made Friday night plans. Most likely we would pick a bar downtown and a few hours later congregate there for beers to wash away the week's tension and begin our weekend fun. It was April, the last of the snow was melting from the sun's warmth, and mud was thick and oozy.

One friend suggested an adventure to Humpty, my family's cabin in the mountains, for an impromptu barbeque. Within moments, we agreed that it was a brilliant idea.

Folks were tired of the downtown jaunts and wanted to mark the beginning of spring with something different. The cabin was only a half-hour drive from campus and a few of us had cars.

In the early evening, twelve of us piled into just two cars and found our way up the mud-slicked, pot-holed road to the cabin. We were equipped with various barbeque fixings and ice-cold six packs of beer. Fortunately, the propane tank still had some gas, and thus did not thwart our dreams of dogs and burgers hot from the grill. The beer started flowing and the spirit of merriment grew. This cabin escape far from campus took place two weeks before final exams and felt like the perfect way to relax and celebrate spring, even if only for an evening.

We laughed, talked, and filled our bellies with flame-cooked food complemented by plenty of chips and beer. As the clock moved close to midnight, we made the collective decision that it was time to pile back into the two cars and return to campus. Our designated drivers jingled their keys to signal us all that it was time to go. Sports games and studying would await us in the morning.

It was dark with only a sliver of moon showing under a sprinkling of stars when we headed back up the path to our vehicles. One car had managed to become stuck in the thick mud and we all got out intending to push it free when we noticed that the other car was heading straight down the hill toward the pond. We stood in a line dumbfounded, feet oozing in mud, and we watched the right hand blinker go on just before the vehicle plunged into the water with a loud splash. The car had maneuvered around the bank and gone down into the pond's shallow end; its back end faced the center of the pond and the front end aimed its nose toward the bank.

We ran from the top of the hill at warp speed toward the car and met one of our gang stumbling out of the front seat, seemingly clueless and clearly disoriented as to where he was or what had happened. Our designated driver was drunk. There was lots of "what were you thinking...what the heck...and then, of course, what do we do now?!" The owner of the car, actually the student whose vacationing parents had kindly lent her their car, was the only partygoer who was rendered speechless. That person was yours truly and the car belonged to my parents.

Late as it was on this dark night, we knew there was little chance we could resolve this unfortunate situation immediately. Returning to the other car, we decided it would be best for someone to take the inebriated friend back to campus and to return with clothing for everyone else to stay and sleep at Humpty. That night a lot of loud snoring was heard echoing from the sleepers in the loft, on the floors, and draped across the old couches in the front room. We were bundled in smelly clothes that the boys had gathered from dorm rooms and returned for our use. The temperatures had dipped and the pot-bellied stove had begun to lose its fire. We snuggled to stay warm and hoped for some sleep before we had to face the next day.

Come morning the car was towed successfully out of the pond, but not without challenges and payment of a hefty fee to the tow truck man who initially declared that retrieval would be near impossible. Then there were the additional garage fees to fix a few damaged things. Finally, there was the daunting dilemma of precisely how to tell my parents: the biggest challenge of all. Despite repeated advice from my peers to keep the mishap quiet, a voice in my ear insistently pounded its own refrain, "Always tell the truth, no matter how bad; always tell the truth." This had been successfully drilled into me from birth forward, but offered little solace as I listened to the otherwise unanimous advice, "Don't tell the rents."

In the end, I could not lie, but I I could not seem to get the words out either. After picking my parents up at the airport, we all went to dinner at the local Howard Johnson's restaurant for an "all you can eat fried clams" dinner. My brother Steve kept kicking me under the table trying to prompt me to tell, but that "right" moment never came as I gazed at my parents' post-vacation glow. Finally, Steve was the one who mustered up the courage to tell my parents the true story. My dad laughed hard when he heard my tale of woe. Dad had been quite a prankster in college and he actually seemed to appreciate the shenanigans of youth. My mom demonstrated a more motherly approach and responded with, "Someone could have been killed; what were you thinking going up there and drinking?" My dad however, wanted to meet the young man who took his car for a swim; although I thought that my dad would be the last person this boy would want to meet.

For several months after the incident, this boy endured friends calling him "Crash." But Crash was a shy, unassuming person and one whom you would least expect to do something as reckless as this. For him, the nickname appeared to be pure torture.

About a year later, my parents were on campus for a college

event and my dad mentioned that he never did meet the young man who drove his car into Humpty's pond. I spied the boy across the green talking with a few other students and walked over to introduce him. My dad just grinned, extended his hand in greeting, and simply said, "Hi Crash, great to meet you. I'm Mr. Caswell."

This incident allowed me to get to know another part of my dad that made him so real and even more special to me. He understood that life did not always go as well as planned, and that it's how we handle challenging moments that teach the greatest lessons. And those are the ones that stick.

# A Fine Resting Place

*O*ne particularly mild Thanksgiving, twenty-five years
after my dad's death, I took a walk around the property
alone. I wandered near the old cellar hole where a century
ago a farmhouse had stood. I visited the nearby graves of two
young children, whom I suspected might have died from one of
that era's epidemic diseases. I traversed across the field to my
favorite waterfall where the water rushes over a steep ledge and
pours into a big pool below. I sat there on my perfect perch and
thought of all the times I had followed the stream, rock by rock,
carefully stepping to avoid falling in the water. I played a game
as a child when I wanted to escape and to be alone in nature. All
worries dropped away and nothing else mattered as I tripped
down the stream, branches brushing against my face; the only
sound was the rush of water.

My walk ended at the dog's graveyard, which was a spot
situated just above an aging, moss-covered tennis court. The
lines were barely visible but the court was still playable.
There were six graves: one for each of our family dogs whose
final hunting ground was always Humpty. They had filled
our families' lives with affection. I stopped at each gravesite,
each one marked with a large rock carried from the property
and etched with the pet's name. First, I visited Moose, whose
grave was closest to the stream. He was my youngest brother's
family dog, a large chocolate Lab with a bundle of energy, and
a personality similar to the famed dog from the book "Marley

and Me." Next to Moose was Bentley, a gentle beauty of a golden retriever. My brother had given this dog to his bride on their wedding day, tying the puppy to the post as she entered the wedding reception. Then there was Baron, my first and most beloved dog. My husband, then boyfriend, had given me a small box on my birthday and I hoped that this might be the long-awaited proposal. Instead, I found a small photo of a Chesapeake puppy gazing up at me. Tears of joy flowed and somehow I knew that the proposal was "written" on the pup's face. Baron was paralyzed and died at six-years-young, but in those six years she brought us a lifetime of joy and was what many people referred to as our first child. Next to Baron rested Sally, our beloved black Lab. We had adopted her from a Japanese family who needed to return to Japan. Sally was with us for twelve years, and was as gentle as a lamb; she never even seemed to know how to bark. Then there was Timber, the family golden that my parents adopted when we older kids went off to college and my younger sister was left at home without other siblings around. Timber could hold three tennis balls in her mouth and smile. Then there was Happy, the black Lab that loved and helped shepherd me through adolescence. I remember that the family couldn't easily agree a name for her, until at last we decided on Happy, a perfectly fitting name for a Labrador. Lastly, my oldest brother Stephen had recently lost his dog of 15 years, Linden. And I expected that Linden too would join our gang of beloved canine companions laid to rest on the hill.

So on this quiet Thanksgiving woodland walk, I sat and gazed at this line-up of wonderful dogs, and was grateful for all of the love and affection they had brought into our lives. I admired the beautiful resting place they had next to the brook shaded by large pine trees. Then I stood ready to return and rejoin our Thanksgiving family gathering.

As I approached the cabin, I heard my husband's voice sharing stories with my brother about last year's escapades at deer camp. The wind whistled through the pine trees and Humpty was brimming with family, memories, and stories. My father would be happy to know how much we still enjoy being at Humpty – a place that once had seemed to be just a quiet parcel of land was now full of life. Humpty is my father's living legacy, and this cozy rustic cabin in the woods holds much more than just a lifetime of memories.

# Dog Lessons

$\mathcal{T}$he popular book *Marley and Me* is a story about life and love and the world's worst dog. My mother and my husband both gave the book to me for my fiftieth birthday. It was a compliment that the two people who knew me best understood the depth of my lifelong love affair with dogs. Reading *Marley and Me* had me laughing well into the wee hours of the night and a steady flow of tears had fallen upon my cheeks by its finish. I lent the book to friends who shared a devotion to dogs. One Sunday evening, I dropped by my friend John's home unexpectedly to pick up the book. He opened the door and when he saw me, he turned a bit ashen. He stammered, swayed, and called for his wife Lynda. Perplexed, I stood still in their entryway and wondered what might be wrong.

Apparently, their young pup had gone into one of the backpacks that was lying on the living room floor, maneuvered the book out, and happily chomped on the front cover until he was discovered. John and Lynda had noticed the book's inscription ( it was the copy from my mother), which dashed any hope for a quick and easy replacement. I looked at the dog-eared book that now had a sizable bite taken from the cover, removed the book from John's hands, and assured them both that there was no need to replace the book. I would continue to treasure it knowing that it now was truly "one of a kind," and the book had its very dog own story.

As children, we traveled to my grandparents' large white house every Sunday. My grandparents raised black Labradors and we would play with each new batch of pups, and watched the dogs grow up and older. Topsy and Mopsy were two of my favorites because they loved to follow us around the bramble paths when we played hide and seek. And then my own parents had four family dogs when we were growing up. First, there was Mickey, then Frannie, Happy, and finally Timber. Wherever we were, home had a dog.

There was one stretch of time after college when I didn't have a dog. On one occasion, we were gathered at Humpty for a birthday celebration when my then boyfriend, now husband, presented me with a small box shaped like a ring box. Opening it, I did not find a ring...but I did find a photo of a Chesapeake Bay retriever puppy. I smiled and took this as a good omen because I thought that a boy does not usually give a dog as a gift without long-term intentions.

We named our "Chessie" Baron and he became the first dog that I could truly call my own. Our Baron was only six when he became paralyzed. Sadly, and rather ironically, Baron died on the day that Christopher Reeves fell off his horse and was paralyzed too. One morning I had found Baron lying on the floor and unable to move. It was 4:30a.m. and I was in hysterics. I called my good friend, Chris, chief of the Charlotte Rescue Squad, and requested an ambulance. He showed up at our door with a large wool blanket, helped us carry Baron to the car, and calmed me down. A few hours later, after multiple assurances from the vet that it truly was the best decision for the dog, we had Baron "put to sleep." He lived a short life, but he lived a good life when measured by the countless adventures and the mountains of fun that we had together.

Sally, a black Labrador, came into our lives a year later. A Japanese family had raised her for a year, but now they were looking for a good home for Sally because they needed to relocate to Japan. Sally was as thin as a greyhound and not that attractive to look at, but nonetheless, I fell in love with her immediately. During her twelve years with us, she was sweet, loyal, considerate, and always ready to play. She watched my two little girls grow up.

The day we were to put our aged Sally to rest was bittersweet. We cried, we laughed, and we cried again. My husband Tim took Sally for a long walk on our land and fed her steak for lunch. Sally basked in the sunshine while Tim dug a grave next to the five other past family pets at our beloved mountain retreat, Humpty. Back at the cabin, several close friends and family dropped by and surrounded her with love. We took photos. We buried our faces deeply into her fur. I sensed she knew these were her final hours and she accepted all our love and attention with dignity. My husband and I buried Sally in a light rain at dusk under an umbrella of tall pine trees. Now she was laid to rest among all the other family dogs at Humpty with its majestic view of Camel's Hump and the calming sounds of a nearby brook.

Dogs have been such an important part of my life and family. They help to remind me to be in the moment. I notice little things more when out on early morning and late night walks with my four-footed companions. Dogs slow my pace; they tug the leash as we go down our road, offering continual reminders to make many stops, sniff the roses, the grasses, the breeze, and don't forget to pee. Dog-led walks create opportunities for keen observation such as noticing the color and texture of curling bark on a birch tree or the beating wings of a hummingbird gathering nectar from a hollyhock. They teach us patience and perseverance. Throw a ball to a dog and you'll see that most dogs never want to give up and will continue exuberantly until they are truly dog-tired and ready to drop! Dogs teach us joy and playfulness. Anyone who has witnessed a dog lying in the grass, sprawled on its back with all four legs sticking straight up in the air, and wiggling its body in unselfconscious delight can attest to this. Dogs also bring us comfort. I cannot count the transformative moments when I was mad at the world and needed a steadfast friend; whenever I would nuzzle my weary face into my dog's furry neck I could count on receiving the lick of a great and slobbery kiss.

Dogs can drive us crazy too with their naughty antics. Once my mother left a plate of pork chops on the kitchen counter only to return to an empty plate; however, later that evening each one of us found a gnarly, nibbled pork chop left under our pillows...

As I finish this story and I am looking down at my faithful friend Maggie, a two-year-old Lab and dog number seven, I know that I can count on her for many more sloppy kisses and biscuits of wisdom.

# A Wish for Quiet

$\mathcal{I}$t takes only moments to find simplicity when the power goes out: suddenly everything turns off and all is quiet. One evening my twelve-year-old daughter Kate and I were sitting on my bed watching one of her favorite videos. In preparation for dinner, I had just turned the burner on the kitchen stove to warm onion soup. In the oven were frozen meatballs rolling next to big chunks of orange sweet potato seasoned with olive oil, pepper, and salt. My husband had brought home a French baguette and returned outside to shovel the heavy snow from the walk.

Suddenly we heard a loud pop, saw a flash of fire in the sky, and then were immersed in darkness. It wasn't a total surprise that we lost power that night, as all day long we had watched the tree branches dip closer to the ground under a heavy blanket of wet fallen snow. I had heard reports that my neighbor's husband was stranded in Philadelphia. Earlier in the day, my sister Annie had called from the island of St. Thomas to inform me of her flight delays – uncertain whether the plane would even depart. She and Larry, her significant other, were traveling north to have fun in the snow. I let her know that her timing for that was perfect. Throughout the day, my daughter expressed her disappointment regarding the postponement of our own plans to travel to Boston. Other winter-hardy friends called repeatedly to entice us to brave the road conditions and travel to Stowe for some winter fun.

But in those first few moments of darkness, we scurried to

find candles. I was grateful that the soup had warmed enough to satisfy. For me, the quiet by a warm fire sipping soup with a dog at my feet was sheer bliss. We had only one flashlight that cast a dim glow, but fortunately, we had countless candles. The house felt warm from the steady wood fire that had burned all day. My daughter located the small reading light attached to the music stand and was immersed in a book all day.

I embraced the darkness and quiet, and I relished the fact that my laptop still had fifty-five percent power so that I could continue to write. I recognized the irony…

But when the power goes out, all of the gadgets, televisions, phones, and computers are useless. Eventually the batteries wear down and you are left with the candles' glow.

I smile and watch my daughter read with her head buried in her book, captured by the story that has held her all day. My black Lab puppy Maggie is stretched out by the woodstove snoozing, truly dog-tired from a serious romp around the neighborhood in deep drifts of snow. Outside, all of the houses look dark. The only light is the natural reflection of a white snow-laden landscape.

We all wonder how long this storm and serene state will last; I secretly hope that it will take a long time for the power to return. I like this enforced simplicity because it stills all our plans and we focus instead on primal needs for shelter, warmth, and food. My husband has brought in enough dry wood to last the night and the cupboards have enough food to last for days. We have Scrabble and Monopoly on the living room floor.

On one of our kitchen cabinet doors is a drawing that my oldest daughter made when she was eight. She is now fifteen-years-old. Through all the years, when other drawings were regularly put up and then taken down, I could never bring myself to remove this particular one. It is a stick figure drawing of a person saying, "I wish for quiet."

On this wonderful dark and snowy night, I did get my wish for quiet, hours of candlelight, and a snoring sleepy dog too.

# Suitor's Feet

*M*y grandmother was a Southern belle. Her house was filled with stories and beautiful memorabilia. Her silver rested in an old chest that had been buried beneath her granddaddy's home during the Civil War. When the war ended, it was dug up and passed down through the generations. She had a piano that had been played by Generals Grant and Lee. Years later, the treasured grand was destroyed by fire when it was placed in storage during her transition move, when she traded south for north.

As a child I loved to snuggle my face deep into my grandmother's mink fur coat during the church sermon and smell the sweetness of her Joy perfume and feel the softness of her slender hands clasped around mine. I often slept over at her house. In the morning, I would get up early and go stand by her bed and watch her sleep. I'd stare at her flowing, curly grey hair. She'd waken and ask me to get her hairpins and the silver mirror on her dresser and then I would watch her twist her soft curls into a bun and they'd disappear. She had a large framed collage that hung beside her bed that held photographs of some of the men in her life that had once come courting; I'd point and ask her to tell me the story of one particular man, the man with the ugly feet.

She would take my hand, smile, and begin the story that I knew by heart. There was once a man with whom my grandmother was quite smitten, and he was hinting of marriage. One day when they were walking barefoot along the beach, she glanced down at his feet. She was aghast. He had the most awful, thorny, misshapen feet she had ever seen. From that day forward, the sound of wedding bells was muffled forever. I still wonder if he ever knew and understood that he never had a chance with my Nana because of those feet.

For my grandmother, things always came around to feet. When my siblings or I brought dates over for dinner, we sat at her elegant table with silver spoons and garnished plates. She held court here, talking nonstop in her charming Southern lilt. You couldn't help but listen. She engaged us in conversations about politics and current events, and eventually, diplomatically, or not, she probed our guests with personal questions.

We tried so carefully to steer those lively conversations away from feet. Often, we were reticent to leave the table for even a few minutes to visit the powder room; we were always uncertain of what might transpire in our absence.

After dinner, we'd retreat to the living room for brandy and dessert. We'd attempt to direct her to the piano and flatter her so that she'd play for us, hoping the music would distract her. Yet despite our best tactics and plans, the inevitable found its way into every evening. She would say, "So, how are your feet?" She would say it in a way that would almost sound as though it were a normal part of conversation. Somehow, with her abundant Southern charm she would maneuver our dates into removing their socks and shoes for inspection before the night was through. Our faces reddened and we vowed once more that this would be the last date we would ever bring to our grandmother's house.

So there we would be sitting in her living room adorned with antiques and oriental rugs, and our grandmother's smiling brown eyes gazing at our dates' bare feet. We would sink deeper into our chairs awash in humiliation. In due time and much to our surprise, many dates found this situation quite humorous, and they were non-plussed, jocular, and happy to oblige.

My brother once endured an uncomfortable evening because his date's feet were not attractive. During dinner, his eyes began to well with tears in anticipation of the inevitable call for a viewing of her feet. However, grandmother gave my brother and his date an unexpected reprieve: she did not ask. However, she did comment on the girl's pretty face.

In time, we resigned ourselves to and accepted our grandmother's odd fascination with feet. We also began warning our dates.

# The Best Couch in Beantown

*I* have made twelve love matches in a span of twenty years, and all of the couples are still married. Whenever I come across a happy pair, I often ask them how they met. This question often brings a smile or look whereby you know that they are trying to decipher cues about who is going to tell the story this time. Usually she starts, and by the time the story ends, I find I have heard a most interesting account of how two people first began their journey into love. Rarely have I found a "how-we-met" story dull. Many have given me goose bumps and a few have brought me to tears. I'd love to share a few "how-they-met" stories from my own collection of matches.

Boston was the backdrop for my first successful match. My roommate Caroline and I shared a flat in the upscale Beacon Hill section. Caroline was a smart, interesting, and attractive woman with a sweet smile. During this time, one of my close male friends, Sandy, was doing a residency in Boston and about once every month he spent the night on our living room couch. He was grateful for the free bed and for the company of two single women. We three had great fun together lingering over meals and late evening talks.

One night Caroline came home after having experienced another dreadful-date-from-hell and sat on my bed in tears. Trying to comfort her, I asked if she had ever considered dating Sandy. She looked at me, tilted her head, and repeated his name several times. I nodded and reminded her that he was the attractive, smart, and nice guy who slept on our couch every few weeks. I am not sure if I was responsible for her epiphany, however, within a few weeks they were an item, and within a few months they were engaged. I was celebrated as a matchmaking hero with all of the respective happy parents.

This marked the beginning of a long series of surprisingly successful matches.

Another match took place at Tuckerman's Ravine in New Hampshire's White Mountains, a well- known east coast adventure skiers' spring Mecca. A group of us was headed there to climb up Mount Washington with our skis and schuss down the ravine's steep terrain. My friend Anne and I "crashed" an available room located near the mountain, which was temporarily vacant because some of the guys we were there to meet had not yet shown up. That was lucky for us because we had not booked any accommodations for ourselves. As we lay there with our sleeping bags pulled up to our chins, I told her that I thought that she and Donnie, one of the gents soon to arrive, would in fact make a good match. She was divorced and was ready to meet a new man.

We knew that the guys would arrive eventually, and we assumed that then we were destined to be perched sleeping in the hallway. They showed up at around three a.m. and mercifully, they let us stay right where we had settled in. By the end of the weekend, Anne and Don had clasped hands; by the end of the year, they were married. We never skied Tuckerman's that weekend as conditions in the ravine were too dangerous, but my friends' romantic match made that little excursion the trip of a lifetime, actually two lifetimes.

A few months later, I invited a male friend to join me for dinner with friends in Burlington's North End. I had relocated to Vermont and for over two years had been living with a man who didn't seem the least bit interested in the "M" word. So, I began thinking about some of the cute single men I knew and somehow landed a quasi-date with a male acquaintance named Davis. As we walked down the steps to a charming Italian restaurant, I spied the group friends we were there to meet waving us over to the table. I noticed an open spot next to a single gal whom I liked a great deal. In that brief moment, I thought that she and Davis would make a much better match. With that in mind, I slipped my escort off my own arm and I slid into the open seat to do my best to exert the power of suggestion. Bingo. The two began dating the following week.

Another matchmaking moment took place at our family cabin, Humpty. One particular evening, a male friend well loosened by a drink or two had asked me if an attractive woman there was attached to the man with whom she had arrived. He had been the fourth man to ask me that same question! I looked into my friend's blurry eyes and said, "If you even want a chance with her, call her first thing on Monday morning." Given his compromised cognitive state, I did not expect that he would remember our conversation at all. But in fact, he did remember, and he had taken my call-on-Monday-morning advice. They were married shortly thereafter.

This fondness for matchmaking has continued, as has my fascination with finding out how couples first meet. It has been heartwarming and fun to play my small part in helping people to find their soul mates. I love to bring people together, in friendship, in partnership, or in love. And now you have been fairly warned: I'm always on the lookout for good "how-we-met" stories and good matchmaking connections.

# Slithery Snakes and Classmates

*E*veryone usually remembers their first kiss. I remember mine, and it was not your usual first kiss. It involved a garage, a slithery green snake, and a seven-year-old boy. I had not thought about that moment in a long time, but one evening my husband Tim and I spontaneously decided to go to our high school reunions at a downtown bar. The weather was good and the reunion included both our high school classes. Upon arriving at the popular watering hole, a band was playing in the outdoor courtyard, and I was very surprised to be greeted by a boisterous voice saying, "Hey, the first girl I ever kissed." I was taken by complete surprise: there was the boy, now grown man, who once stood in that garage on the other side of my first lip smack. The memory of that childhood moment came reeling back. And there standing before me was a glimpse of the boy, now transformed into a tall blond man with blue eyes and a nice smile. I laughed and gave him a hug and soon we were deep in conversation catching up on our lives. It turned out that now he lived one town away from mine and we shopped at the same market.

When we were children he had lived just two doors away from my childhood home. Somehow, on one particular afternoon we had both ended up in his garage together. His older brother had found a long green snake with yellow eyes, and he held it menacingly just outside the garage door. He threatened us saying that unless we kissed each other on the lips he would let the snake loose on us. Terrified, I turned to the other boy and kissed him quickly on the lips, hoping that the snake would disappear and that the garage door would be open.

Now flashing forward thirty-five years to this evening, Tim and I strained to be heard over the loud music. We talked with many other people we hadn't seen in more than thirty years. People greeted each other with warmth and enthusiasm. A handful of men introduced themselves with an additional comment stating how much heavier they were since their glory days, always related with a small sheepish smile; the women who had gained weight since high school years didn't step forward or sheepishly smile to explain. There was a spirit of camaraderie in the group as people hugged and greeted one another as if they had all been the best of buddies. It didn't seem to matter whether you were a jock or part of the popular "under the stairs" gang or a loner. What mattered was that you were all together during the teen years sharing the same experience, and that now you had mustered up the courage and gumption to show up and walk down memory lane. Tim and I hadn't really given the occasion much forethought before we decided to attend, but later I realized that the thought of attending any reunion can be terrifying – it can bring out all sorts of new and old wounds or insecurities.

One classmate had traveled quite far to attend and beamed with pride as he shared the story of how he had just given his wife a vintage Ford Mustang for their anniversary. Another person shared that she was moving through a difficult divorce and was happy to see so many classmates from her earlier days. Throughout the evening stories were reeled in and out about children in college, and now some were even accounts of life as grandparents. The stories flowed as the beer filled the glasses and loud music filled the room.

Glancing over at Tim, I could see he was having a great time, telling stories and reminiscing about some of the good old days. When I approached him to give him the "fifteen-minutes-to-go" warning, usually his role, his friend pulled me closer and began to recite the story of the cop car and the apples; Tim had gotten into serious trouble when they were age fifteen for throwing rotten apples at a cop's car. I laughed as much as ever at this story, which had been retold many times, as it was one of the ones that my teenage daughters had latched onto and often requested retellings.

My voice was beginning to get hoarse as I'd had enough of trying to talk over the loud music, and so I escaped outside, found a table, and listened to the band play light jazz. I was happy to be alone with my thoughts, and it didn't matter how long it took for Tim to join me. About half an hour passed before he came out and was ready to leave. We walked to the car together lost in our silent reveries. Once on the road, Tim turned to me and asked, "Do I still look ok?" I looked back at him and smiled. "You look great bud, and I'm glad that I'm with you." We drove home together and I think that we almost held hands.

The next day we were off to pick up our youngest daughter Kate after two weeks at sleep-away camp. I was looking forward to a family movie night together, and was glad that Tim and I had both so easily survived our previous evening's start of the high school reunion. Tonight would be the official gathering at a nearby hotel. I had no regrets about missing that gathering because I had indeed held onto the best of my high school years – my husband Tim.

# Skinny Dipping with Loons

*A*loon calls in the distance. Eerie and shrill, another loon answers. If you have heard a loon's call deep in the night, you know it sounds like a wail. The sound can be simultaneously beautiful, plaintive, and haunting. There is more than one call, and at one point in my life, I knew each one – the wail, the tremolo, the yodel, and the hoot – and I knew what each call meant. Some people may have called me loon obsessive.

Friends and family gave me thematic gifts filled with loon images: loon mugs, t-shirts, albums, books, statues, and even loon-y pencil sharpeners. For several months, my phone's answering machine even had the recorded sound of a loon's call, until several friends complained and said it sounded like someone was being murdered. My gift-bearing friends didn't understand that my love of loons wasn't about loon stuff, but was about the birds and their habitats: unspoiled and peaceful wilderness. Loons, and I, are most content in such places.

For many summers now, I have had the pleasure of visiting friends with homes on five different serene lakes scattered throughout New England. At each place there is the shared wonder of resident loons and I wake and sleep to the sound of their calls.

One summer while visiting dear friends at one of these treasured spots, an island at Squam Lake, I swam very close to a loon, tread water for at least ten minutes, and watched until it finally fanned its white and black wings out and skimmed across the top of the water in exquisite flight.

This annual visit includes celebrating my goddaughter Tashi's birthday. Tashi lives in Switzerland with her family and makes this trip but once a year. During this year's trip to Squam Lake, I also kayaked around the island and watched loons bathing in the coves. A few swimmers bobbed from rock to rock with squeals of laughter, pure and simple fun. It felt like this was a glimpse of earlier days, life before the pace had sped up so much. Many of us now seek refuge and havens away from everyday life's racing tempo and the tempting "garden" of Apples, iPods, Blackberries, etc. But today I sat for a long time with my paddles still, enjoying and observing something lovely, enduring, and ageless.

Every morning, I wake up early on the island. Because I am only there for a few days, I want every moment to count. The loons wake me with their call from the far cove – this is the same cove where the boat crashed in the Katharine Hepburn and Henry Fonda movie classic *On Golden Pond*. I dress and go to the dock with my pen, pad, and camera hoping to catch a glimpse of these ancient birds. They are among the oldest species in North America, and in fact, they are one of the oldest species on earth. As I sit quietly waiting to hear another call, I often hear the hum of boat engines not far off in the distance. On the dock my back is warmed by the sun and I feel somewhat like a clay pot baking. I embrace the warmth knowing that the air and water will soon cool me down. Other bird sounds fill the dense forest of thick brush. I wonder what this place was like before humans arrived. After the loons stopped calling, I become more aware of the other birds' chatter as they are waking up to this new day. I am relaxed and feel miles away from any distractions. Water ripples radiate near me from time to time, and I see small fish swimming at the bottom searching for food. Wisps of lake grass poke upward toward the sky, drinking in the sun, like me.

With the day now awake, it won't be long before our morning dip. I spy my friend Sus coming to join me on the dock for our morning ritual. We have moved forward in age, and our trips to the private cove where we navigated rocks and occasional fisherman to make our suit-less dips have been replaced with slightly more daring adventures. Now we slip our unadorned bodies down into the lake in close proximity of the early morning coffee drinkers on the nearby dock. When the coast is clear, we splash in alone and free. We swim carefully amongst the large boulders underneath the surface, and we move the water slowly with our hands, while we talk and share our last year's secrets and stories. We talk about what we are learning, what we are becoming, and about watching our children move closer to young adulthood. We cherish our yearly ritual together and decades of close friendship. It's easy to seamlessly pick our conversations right up from where we left off the year before; it's hardest that our time together is so brief. Sus and I share an open spirit and we embrace life fully.

I spy a loon swimming just ahead. We grow quiet and watch as it moves peacefully and then flutters its expansive wings for just a moment. It must sense our nearness but remains a little longer, and allows us to enjoy its company. We are together on this peaceful lake where the only sounds are the ripples moving over the rocks and us. The loon then extends its wings fully and prepares for flight. It takes off low across the water's surface, flying just inches above the ripples, then rises, and disappears into a distant cove. I smile thinking that here I am swimming naked with my best friend and a loon in this magical place we share once every year.

Each summer when I hear the first loon's call, the sound summons my feelings of connection with all that remains wild and unspoiled, and I am reminded that in these places humans are visitors blessed to witness and experience such untouched beauty and grandeur.

# Rainbows and Heron

*I* could not help but glance at the rainbow on my left as I traveled south down the interstate highway that divides the Green Mountains from the Adirondacks. With every turn, the road ahead appeared increasingly wet, indicating a recent shower, and with each sidelong glance the rainbow appeared to beam brighter. Soon I noticed a faint second rainbow appeared above the first, and one became a perfect arch. I had never witnessed a rainbow so bright and so perfect.

I'd been thinking about my dad this entire drive. It was his birthday and I hadn't seen him in thirty years. He was fifty-four when he died from cancer, and this year I felt particularly nostalgic. I had recently turned fifty-four.

As I watched the merging hues brighten from a soft red, yellow, and blue to deeper colors, I thought of how often we think of those we love in nature, or at least I do. Loons, butterflies, heron, and dragonflies show up in my horizon and seem to kindle remembrances of loved ones who have passed on. I have always believed in reincarnation, of sorts. At Humpty on the night of my wedding rehearsal dinner, a large blue heron flew over the pond and landed in close view of the porch. I was awestruck; I had never seen a heron visit Humpty in all of the forty years we had been there. I remember thinking, "That's dad, bringing his blessings." I felt his presence and his love and whether or not it was really him, or just a sign, it felt as though that heron had brought my dad's blessings to me. My mom once shared that when wintering in Florida she always thought that the blue heron visiting her porch was her mother, my Nana.

I continued to think about my dad on this evening's nostalgic drive down to visit a friend. I didn't really own anything memorable that belonged to my dad, such as a special watch or a pair of binoculars. It had never really occurred to me until this particular moment with a full-arched double rainbow beaming over my head that my dad wasn't really into things. The activities and time he spent with us out in nature was what he loved best and what mattered to him the most. It was his gardening, fishing, or annual Humpty hunting retreats (with lots of card playing and drinks) that mattered. It was maple sugaring in his homemade shack. It was the countless letters he composed to dear friends and family, and the Robert Frost poems he recited at the dinner table that mattered. He did not leave me many "things" when he passed away. What he left me with was gratitude for the beauty of nature and an immense appreciation for the web of human connections; that was my dad, and that was his bequest to me.

As I moved through the following week, and all the days that marked his birthday, his death, and his memorial service (two days apart and thirty years ago), I kept thinking about the beauty of that slowly-arching rainbow gracing my drive and the father that still graces my life.

# Leap of Faith

$\mathcal{T}$here are times in our lives when we take a leap of faith and travel into uncharted territory; a moment when we just hang on to hopes that everything will be fine. I recall doing that a lot during my younger years, especially when it came to travel. I was never good at organizing the trips, but I was always willing to go along. These decisions had me traveling across the country with a college girlfriend in a Volkswagen bug with a two-person tent and her guitar, touring through Europe with a Euro Rail pass and ten dollars a day, and climbing in the Himalayas and sleeping in dirt-floored tea huts at 19,000 feet. In a span of just ten years, my twenties, three trips provided adventures, challenges, and risks, which I survived without too much wear and tear. Looking back, I realize that my travels and the way I chose to travel "on the cheap" shaped much of who I am today. Taking risks, meeting new people, experiencing third world cultures, and traveling alone for a period of time made a huge impact on my perspective of the world.

Not long ago and about twenty years later, my youngest daughter's school bandleader asked me if I would consider chaperoning a middle school band trip to Disneyland. I just about fell off my chair. Although I felt complimented, this invitation was my idea of daunting. I wondered if the bandleader had made a mistake. I certainly hadn't volunteered. Although I had considerable respect for this teacher's music program and the high standards he held for his students, I didn't know him well enough to think that I would be asked to go. I called him back with several good reasons why I felt there were far better choices for this honor. I was sure other parents would welcome this amazing opportunity. But he was prepared and ready to counter my "No thank you" with his reasons why he thought I would be a great chaperone. He flattered me further and stated that he had given considerable thought to which parents would be best suited to chaperone and travel with the band.

Before I could make my decision, a consultation with my daughter was critical. I was sure she would nix me well before I could even finish stating my case. Previously, she had banned me from chaperoning at school dances and had been lukewarm to my participation on class field trips. Therefore, this history seemed like my paid ticket to say "no thanks" in an appropriate and understandable way. However, my daughter delivered an emphatic and resounding "Yes!" instead. She begged me to go. Then she badgered me to inform the bandleader of my decision quickly. A green light from my daughter, wow! Because my daughter was so enthusiastic, I informed the bandleader that if he felt he knew me well enough to think I could do it well, then I would take the chance and go... A few days later, I overheard my daughter excitedly telling a friend that her mom was going to be one of the trip chaperones. Would she still feel that way once we were there, I wondered.

It was an amazing trip. I ran around Disney World at warp speed chasing my gang of five wonderful girls. In the beginning I let them know that I did not intend to go on rides but would happily be the caretaker of their backpacks. Somehow, they successfully coaxed and cajoled me to join them each time. I'd give in, go on the ride, and scream like a banshee in ways I had not done in years. And according to a "benched" chaperone who witnessed my wide-eyed and dazed "Everest" exit, she gave me a high-five and a "You-go-girl"! I finally did say no to one ride, the "Tower of Terror," an elevator that dropped several hundred feet.

We returned to our hotel room each night around 11p.m. My bed was the pullout couch in the center room and eight girls slept in the adjoining rooms. There were always one or two girls up during the night with some issue that interrupted their sleep and consequently, mine too. Occasionally I shared my thin, lumpy pullout mattress and bed (replete with a metal bar placed smack in the middle of the bed frame), with one girl or another. During the night, I hugged the bed's edge, fearful that I might roll onto that metal bar or a child. Sleep was elusive that week.

After five days we headed home. We stumbled into our hometown airport around midnight and were all greeted warmly with hugs from grateful parents. My husband smiled and greeted me with a hug, saying, "You look really tired... but a happy tired."

I finally crawled into my bed at home around 1a.m. Everything in my body ached. As I pulled the covers up, I felt two small arms wrap around me. I turned to see my daughter's smiling face, "Thank you Mommy for coming on the trip. I loved having you part of it." Then she was off in a flash. My weary head hit the pillow with a sense of contentment. "I did it," I said into my fluffy pillow as I stretched my legs out fully on the big soft mattress. I actually did it, I thought.

# The Sidelines

*T*he loud cheering and jingling of bells could be heard from the moment I stepped out of my car in the upper lot of the high school, which is situated in a rural spit of land overlooking the Green Mountains. I found my place on the first row of metal bleachers to watch the final field hockey game of the season. Glancing at the clock, I saw the 0-0 score with eighteen minutes left in the first half. Bundled in mittens, hats, and blankets draped over our legs, the regular crowd had gathered. With boisterous cheers and yells, the sideliners, namely the parents, hollered strategy tips to the players and positive reinforcements such as "nice pass" or "good block."

I spied my daughter in her uniform with its big number one printed on the jersey, a right-wing offensive player scurrying up the field. The two women sitting next to me commented on her speed and agility, and I found myself grinning slightly. She certainly didn't get it from me. Just hours earlier I had tucked a SKOR chocolate bar into her bag and I'd said with a smile, "Score one today." She looked at me with that teenage look, "Ok Mom." I didn't usually say things like that but it was the last game of the season I thought, well, why not.

A few minutes before the first half of the game ended, our team scored and the crowd cheered. We moved into the second half and the three seasoned field hockey moms shivering next to me commented again on my daughter's skill. Shifting my attention back to the game, I watched my girl in her number one jersey take the ball from one end of the field and dribble down the entire length with agility and speed. She took a shot and the next thing I knew we were all screaming the word we love…goal! I found myself jumping up and down and hugging these women that I barely knew. My daughter had scored her first goal of the season!

We all cheered and rubbed our hands together to stay warm. We watched the sun dip lower, the autumn wind swirl, and the time dwindle on the clock. This is my "sideline community," the parents I greet every fall from the sidelines of the high school field hockey field. We all yell, scream, and beam with pride as our girls run back and forth with sticks. Post game we share hot dogs on the grill and rehash the plays. The camaraderie is sweet. I love sharing this part of the day with parents that I get to know better and better each year. My sideline community is one of seven communities that make up my life.

One afternoon while sitting on a picnic bench waiting for a meeting to commence, a person with a familiar face waved as she walked by. She smiled and said, "We miss seeing you in yoga class. Hope you'll join us again soon." I smiled back and thought to myself how much I missed my yoga community. She had been the second person that week who noticed my absence. It made me feel good to be missed and I promised that in the coming weeks I would find my way back to what had once been a regular ritual.

For seventeen years, I have been part of a book group that has met every month to read and share our opinions on all kinds of books: from the latest fiction to classics. We rotate meetings around to each other's homes where we enjoy a hearty meal and lively conversation. We eventually talk about the book, and we often do not agree. We have helped support one another through cancer treatments, divorces, and child-rearing challenges. Most recently, one of our longtime treasured members relocated to a small village in the south of France and our group really felt this loss. I can't image life without my book group, it has brought me the comfort of good friends and good books.

My work community greets me every day with positive and lively energy, as we tackle myriad to-do lists together. We're a team. The organizational culture I work in clearly makes you feel like a family. A bond is nurtured through mutual respect and a passion for the work we do. We all work together to help children and adults succeed in learning. It's an organization that I feel proud to work with, and it is a community of people with whom I feel blessed to share my days.

At the local community college, I have been teaching the same class for eight years and love the students that I strive to inspire each term. I feel I learn as much from them as they may learn from me. In a class entitled Community and Work Experience, students do eighty hours interning at an organization in their field. Students at this thriving community college come from many countries, including Africa, Bangladesh, Croatia, India, and South Vietnam – quite a medley of cultures. One student came to Vermont just after Hurricane Katrina and shared firsthand what it was like the day the storm hit. I enjoy the opportunity to be part of their lives every two weeks for a few hours.

Family and friends are a huge part of my community and I look forward to the many family gatherings and rituals that take place during the year. On one occasion, we had no hot water or heat at home and we spent those few days with friends. It was fun to take part in their daily routines and take advantage of their proximity to wonderful walking trails for my dog Maggie. I also loved walking into town for a refreshing smoothie at the local café. We shared meals together, talked politics, and helped my friend prepare for a class she was teaching that particular evening. On another occasion, an obliging friend literally drove me around all day when my car was in the shop. We also managed to take a long walk and caught up on our lives. I went with her to drop her kids off at school and pick them up again later, and I got a small taste of her weekly routine. During times like these, I feel grateful to be able to turn to and count on friends for help or support. For most of us, our families are our terra firma. Despite our differences (and there clearly are many when it comes to families), we are bound by blood and we are generally there for each other when the road gets bumpy. I can't imagine life without my family and friends.

The town I live in is my larger community where there is ever-present activity in that keeps it vibrant and engaging. I see my neighbors at the local market or coffee shop. Our library is another central place for folks to congregate. We vote together on Election Day, we gather for the annual holiday stroll to sing around the tree, and we ride a float or catch candy at the annual Halloween parade. We mingle and visit during the summer farmers market and sample the amazing array of locally grown foods. We attend village plays and concerts, as well as soccer, baseball and field hockey games.

These many small circles of community make my life vibrant and full. And although I do sometimes still sit on the sidelines to cheer, I don't really sit on the sidelines at all.

# Simple Gifts

*A* week before Thanksgiving my mother visited a local store to purchase a small Thanksgiving treat for her grandchildren. The store was filled to the brim with chocolate Santas and other Christmas treats. Tracking down a store clerk, she inquired as to whether they had any Thanksgiving treats such as chocolate turkeys. The clerk replied enthusiastically that she was certain that there was a large box of them out back. She returned moments later with several chocolate turkeys tied with an orange ribbon. My mom smiled and said thank you. Several days later I returned to the same store to find a large basket of chocolate turkeys prominently displayed on the counter. I wondered if my mom's visit had reminded them that Thanksgiving was on the horizon, and that perhaps the chocolate Santa's could wait another week.

Every year I find myself feeling more like the *Grinch* as I maneuver through what used to be a much warmer and cozier holiday filled with traditions and simple gifts. Now, starting sometime in early November, you begin to see town evergreen trees lit and glowing Santas waving from sleighs. The frenzied pace begins along with the wish lists and the holiday shopping traffic; it all makes me long for simpler times. It is the rituals and the family traditions that stand out in my mind the most. They are what are most remembered and meaningful – yet they sometimes feel squeezed with all of the frenzy.

Last Christmas, a close friend called me to ask if I would like to go to dinner and a show. She suggested that we dress up and make it a special evening. Once seated, we raised our glasses of sparkling bubbly in a toast to our friendship and to each other. She said "Happy Holidays" and went on to tell me that spending time together was the best gift she could imagine. We had a fabulous time laughing and telling stories. The performance was creative and fun. It was an evening I will remember, a gift of time and friendship.

Through the years, my two daughters have become more thoughtful in their gift giving. They make a point of writing a story or a poem, giving me candles or soap, and making themselves available for our family's annual tree cutting ritual. For many years, we have stomped through our property at Humpty to a stand of trees that were planted there by my brother for this very reason. These outings offer lots of interchange about which tree is the choice for this year, although one winter a weather-felled tree made itself our easiest selection.

There were two times in my life when I was far from home during the holidays. Both times I recall yearning to be home with my family. The first occasion was in my early twenties when I was at the mid-point of a European adventure with a friend. We had decided to rent a Swiss chalet and have friends join us for a skiing holiday. I tried to coax my companions to walk two miles to the local village church to attend the Christmas Eve candlelight service, as I could not imagine missing this tradition. With no takers, I contemplated walking there by myself. We had a tree and had purchased small gifts, but it just didn't feel like Christmas to me without attending a service. We went skiing Christmas Eve day and then went out for a small bite to eat. When we returned to our chalet we found our tree adorned in white candles and a small box placed carefully on our table. The box was filled with an assortment of homemade cookies with a note. "Light the candles on the tree and enjoy a few songs together." It was a kind gesture from the Swiss family living downstairs and from whom we had rented the chalet.

So instead of venturing out on the two-mile trek to the village church that evening, I helped to light the candles and sang holiday songs with my gang of friends. We devoured the buttery jam-filled cookies and chocolate, exchanged small gifts, and toasted with champagne.

Ten years later, I found myself flying into Hong Kong with no place to stay. I was on another traveling adventure, this time to Asia and traveling alone. I was determined to keep on schedule and fly from Singapore to Hong Kong despite not having secured accommodations. My mother telephoned early morning to share holiday greetings and to give me the name and number of a friend from church who had a son living in Hong Kong with his wife. Desperate and amazed by this fortuitous stroke of luck, I telephoned them. Less than eight hours later, I was sitting in their flat: blurry-eyed, tired, and grateful. They could tell that I was experiencing a touch of homesickness and I was travel weary, having already been on the road for two months of backpack traveling. I remember that they had asked me how I usually spent the holidays. Trying to hold back tears, I told them about how on Christmas Eve, after the candlelight service, we would come home and have cheese fondue by the fire and read stories. That night my hosts returned home with a bag of groceries. They pulled out a big chunk of cheese and some bread and I could feel a large tear moving down my cheek. We shared a wonderful evening of dipping our long forks into the delicious and gooey cheese while I entertained them with my travel stories. On Christmas Day, we shared a feast at a local restaurant with a group of "expats" and I had so much fun. My family called me and wished me a happy holiday.

The spirit of the season shifted that year as I realized that you can't always be with family and close friends. That year the holiday had been filled with kindnesses extended by complete strangers who were generous and willing to share their home with me as well as share my traditions. Perhaps that is why when I see Santa waving from a sleigh or the town tree ablaze in early November, it bothers me. For me, the best gifts are not always the ones that come wrapped up in ribbons or in a box, but they are gifts from the heart that often appear when we least expect them.

# Taxi Please

*A* decade ago, I overheard a memorable conversation between two forty-something women. I was working out on a treadmill at the local gym, trying to get back in shape and enjoying a brief respite from my two toddler girls. Sweat poured from my forehead as I tried to get my sixty minutes logged in. The two women were nearby and I couldn't help but hear their conversation. I pretended to be reading the open magazine propped on the stand in front of me, which displayed women in stylish outfits with perfect bodies and luscious lips, but I was clearly eavesdropping. The two women were going on and on about a book titled, "Get Out of My Life, but First Could You Drive Me and Cheryl to the Mall." One of the mothers said that all she did was taxi her daughters from place to place and hand them money, otherwise, she said, the teenagers wanted nothing to do with her. She went on to say that her daughters often had her drop them off yards away from their destination. The other woman was nodding her head in agreement, as they continued their rant about teenagers and their raving about this book. I recall thinking naively that my two girls would never grow up to treat me that way. And this book sounded totally absurd. I wondered about what kind of mothers these two women really were, and why they ever bothered to have children.

A few years passed, and I ran into a mother of our favorite babysitter at the farmers market. I exulted about how much we loved her daughter and that she was such a great babysitter and role model for my girls. I told her how lucky she was to have such a wonderful daughter. Her eyes looked at me like a deer in headlights. "Thank you," she smiled. But I read on her face, "If you only knew...just wait until you see what lies ahead with your girls."

When my eldest daughter started high school, I was eager for her undivided attention while riding in the car to and from school to learn more about her life. My "taxi" is a dinged-up minivan strewn with backpacks, shoes, water bottles, and dog hair covered seats (complements of my beloved canine companion and fellow passenger, my black Lab Maggie). The opportunities for undivided attention exists on our drive to and from school, but so do begrudging one word answers to my queries. And yes, these requests are true too, "Please stop here to let me out," (several yards away from the school entrance). And let's not forget these familiar exchanges: "Don't ever come in the building because I'll come out"; "Please don't talk much when my friends are in the car"; "Oh yeah Mom, I want to go the Becca's on Friday night and Adrienne's on Saturday, so could you drop me off and pick me up?," and the follow-up line, "Oh I need money for the movies too." Fortunately, the seven-mile drive to high school takes me by mountain vistas, pastures, and colorful gardens.

I began to realize that my life was now like the ones described by the ranting mothers I had overheard at the health club ten years ago; their descriptions a decade ago perfectly mirror what I experience now.

So I eventually learned that it's not just about the parenting. Teenagers want their space and you are often viewed as the intruder. You do become the unpaid taxi service and the ATM machine. You do need to ask too many questions and you will find yourself feeling like you're an old-fashioned and middle-aged parent. They tell you in unequivocal terms that it is totally not cool to shop in thrift shops. And you begin to get frequent headaches from the music that blares from the car radio, but picking your battles carefully, you listen without too much complaint. Then you are in for another surprise when you begin to find that you actually enjoy some of their music and sometimes tune in even when they are not riding with you.

When my daughter was fifteen, she was invited to go out west on a ski trip with a school buddy and her parents. I liked the parents and was excited for her opportunity to have an adventure. However, as the trip approached, I found myself feeling anxious about her leaving; my worrying grew to the point where I couldn't get anything done. One friend recommended a therapist but most of my friends and colleagues at work said that this was a typical response (parental separation anxiety) and emotion. The day I drove my daughter to the airport I recall handing her the little black suitcase she had carefully packed, her ski bag, and her coat. I didn't say all the motherly cautions I thought I would. I didn't tuck a note in her bag telling her how much I loved her. I simply stood on the curb and watched. With her bags in hand, she turned to go and gave me a kiss on the cheek, "I'll miss you Mom."

On the drive home, I found myself reflecting on that one small parting gesture and statement. For me it was a quintessential teenage moment demonstrating the ebb and flow of raising teenagers and those moments when they show us their paradoxical truth: they really do care and love us, and they are ready to venture a few steps further out into the world to seek their independence and build their own lives.

So now, here I am too – standing aside a little bit more and dropping her off further from the door. Yet I knew that I would need to phone her at least once during this trip, and all that I hoped was that she would be happy to hear from me.

# Krispy Kreme Donuts

One evening, I called my brother to inform him that I was unable to attend the school band's wind ensemble meeting when my sister-in-law's voice interrupted the call.

She wanted to express her disappointment that I'd miss the meeting as she was presenting the plans for the Krispy Kreme fundraiser. She raced through her explanation without pausing for breath, skidded to a full stop, and asked what I thought. My reaction? Why would we encourage consumption of sugarcoated, high-fat donuts in an already obese culture? Why couldn't they sell wreaths or candles or even soap – things that were more useful, meaningful, environmentally friendly, and harmless – but Krispy Kreme donuts?

"Laurie...Are your there?" she said. Without forethought, I blurted out that I didn't know one person that would ever want to purchase Krispy Kreme donuts, and that I had no intention of buying ten boxes, which was the suggested number for each child to sell in order to to reach the overall sales goal. There was a brief pause on the other end and then a quick good bye. I hung up and wondered if I'd come on a little bit too strong. After all, she was trying to raise money for a worthy program.

A few days later, my daughter Kate came home from school waving a yellow paper and wearing a big smile. " Mom, Mom, we're selling Krispy Cremes for wind ensemble, and I need points so if I sell fifteen boxes I can get two points." I could feel myself tighten and realized she was staring at me. "Mom, are you ok?"

"Yes honey, but who are we going to sell that many boxes to? I don't know how we'll even be able to sell ten boxes; my friends don't eat donuts."

She turned to look at me with total puzzlement. "But Mom, why not? Doesn't everyone love donuts?"

That afternoon my friend Hilary and I went for a peaceful walk down a quiet dirt road, sharing our day as our dogs romped along beside us. And with the fresh air and friendship, I tried to tone my indignation down. I checked in with my daughter midway by cell phone, "Honey let's try for ten boxes."

"But Mom – I need points so we are going to have to sell fifteen!"

"Then you figure out who to sell them to," I retorted, and hung up.

A little while later, my cell phone rang. It was Kate. "M-Mom she stammered...I think you are right about selling the donuts. Let's just try for ten boxes."

I wanted to cry. When a pre-teen tells you that you are right about something, well, it's humbling. Perhaps that's because it provokes a flashing reminder of tender moments in your own childhood. Hilary looked bemused as I explained the story to her. Then she asked for my cell phone and dialed.

"Kate, this is Hilary. I just heard about Krispy Kremes. I am so proud of how you handled this situation and how you called your mom and all. Put me down for three boxes." I could hear my daughters excited voice bellow from the phone.

In the end, we sold sixteen boxes of Krispy Kreme donuts and about one-third of the purchasers told us to keep the donuts. They just wanted to support the children and the music program.

Donut delivery day was amazing. We heard Krispy Kreme stories. One person hailed from the South and told us that they'd watch for the Krispy Kreme donut sign to beam bright red, indicating that the donuts were fresh from the oven and piping hot. Apparently, people would literally turn their cars around to stop and grab a hot donut with the warm glaze oozing down over the edge. One of our deliveries was after nine at night. An older gentleman opened the door and promptly reached into the box and took a big bite –much to his wife's horror as she reminded him that he had just brushed his teeth. Another supporter shared a story about the clamor and excitement that occurred even in New York City when Krispy Kreme first arrived. Another family called to say that they had shared their donuts with the milkman, and then they took another box to the local volunteer fire department. My sister-in-law was bringing her box to the local homeless shelter.

A few weeks later, I was enjoying lunch out with the editor of our local town paper and I shared the story of my recent Krispy Kreme donut adventures. She looked straight at me, eyes wide, "Why didn't you call me? I love Krispy Kremes. I would have bought several boxes. The folks at the post office all love them too, so I always bring them some. You know the donuts are legendary; where have you been?" She smiled. In that moment I wondered how I had reached middle age without the slightest notion that Krispy Kreme donuts were a phenomenon with such a devoted following. They were indeed legendary: everyone seemed to be filled with Krispy Kreme memories and stories. I guess that nobody cared that the donuts were dripping with sugar and oozing with fat. They were a treat. One fact that most indulgers agreed upon was that Krispy Kreme were best when eaten hot from the baker's oven, ensuring that the glaze would drip down your chin as you took that first big bite.

That night I snuck down to the freezer and grabbed a Krispy Kreme from the plastic bag in which my daughter had carefully wrapped the several dozen extra donuts. I placed it in the microwave and pushed the start button for eight seconds. The beep sounded embarrassingly loud in the still of the night. I poured myself a big glass of milk and sunk my teeth into my very first hot and oozy Krispy Kreme and wiped the drizzle from my chin.

# Letting Go

*I* barely recognized my friend Anne's voice at the other end of the phone. Between the choppy cell phone connection and the sound of muffled crying, it was difficult to discern her words. In a jumbled and broken message, she was trying to tell me that she had just said good-bye to her eighteen-year-old son who was about to begin his first year at a local college in a few days; she added that she had become lost while driving around the nearby town. I managed to convince her to pull over to the side of the road and calm down. She informed me that she had decided to return home to Boston instead of spending the night with us in Vermont. Part of her wanted our company and to stay, but another part of her sought the four-hour solitary drive home to process emotions and give in to her sadness. For her son, starting college marked the beginning of a new, exciting, and more independent phase of his life. During the past few weeks, I had been watching various parents prepare to send their first child off to college, and I was sympathetic to her emotional state.

I gave her directions to my office and told her we would regroup there. For months, I had been looking forward to our evening out together, and knew that I would try hard to convince her to stay overnight. We'd spend the evening catching up over dinner and then we'd get up at the crack of dawn to go for coffee at Starbucks before she returned home. She came by my office and within a short time, we were both sipping tea by an outside waterfall at a garden center near to where I worked. She shared the weeks of preparation spent to ready her son Ryan for college. Through her stories, it was evident that every member of her family would have their own unique way of adjusting to what life would be like in their home, minus one eldest son.

We then each drove to my house and jumped into one car to venture into my small quaint town, which is filled with wonderful distractions, including little stores and eateries. First, we poked around in the secondhand clothing store trying on clothes, convincing ourselves to make just one purchase each. Next, we headed to the bookstore, we each found a new book, and then we ventured on to the new eco-friendly store. I browsed and my friend put a stainless steel water bottle on the counter, a couple of combination fork/spoons (sporks) and some chocolates. I was perplexed by her purchases – thinking to myself that she must already own plenty of water bottles and utensils by this time. She looked at the store clerk and then at me. She told us that she had sent her son off to college without these items and felt that he would need them. I offered to mail them as I reminded her that she had already said her goodbyes, and then I whisked her off to the restaurant located next door to the shop. Sitting at an outside table with a light breeze, we enjoyed a few glasses of Sauvignon Blanc, salmon salad, and French fries. "So how far is Saint Michael's College from here?" she asked as I finished my last sip of wine. "Oh, only about fifteen minutes or so," I replied.

A few hours later, after returning home to retrieve my sixteen-year-old daughter, we all headed back to see her son Ryan at Saint Michael's campus. She clutched the brown bag that was holding the water bottle, chocolate, and sporks. Ryan had instructed her to meet him in the parking lot. Seeing his dorm room was not offered as an option. Dressed in a white Bob Marley t-shirt, khakis, and a fresh haircut, he smiled when we all piled out of the car. He greeted us, and his mom lovingly handed him the brown bag. My daughter Molly said a brief hello that showed her obvious humiliation that we were even there. With that, he looked at his mother, gave her a brief hug, smiled, and said, "Goodbye Mom, I'm going to be just fine." He stood for a few moments with the bag in hand, watching as we drove away, and I watched my friend bravely holding back her tears. I reached across to put my hand on her shoulder, and said, "You're going to be just fine."

She needed that one more goodbye, and as we drove toward my house, she seemed comforted by the opportunity to have seen him one last time before going home. I reminded her that parents' weekend was only three weeks away. It would take some time for the whole family to adjust to this new chapter. I told her we would invite her son for dinners at our home, and again reminded her that we lived a mere fifteen minutes away from campus.

I glanced in the rear view mirror and caught a glimpse of my sixteen-year-old daughter Molly still dressed in her sweats and t-shirt, and hair in a ponytail from her high school field hockey practice earlier that evening. Only two more years I thought, just two more years until I will find myself in the same position. I only hope that when my time comes I will have someone to comfort me.

# Turquoise Blue Treasures

We arrived on the sandy beach a few hours before dark. Our journey had taken us from four days of crowds, noise, smells, and the horns of New York City to familiar scenery. Weekapaug, a small hamlet of houses situated on the Rhode Island shore, was our annual vacation spot and a family tradition every October. This year we had squeezed in an April visit. My two young daughters, Kate and Molly, sprang from the car before I had even turned off the engine. Out of the car and standing on the beach, I inhaled the sea air and began to feel that familiar calm sweeping over me and filling me with ease. The waves were frothy and wild and I could taste the salt in the air. Kate and Molly were already running toward the surf when I glanced down and spied a blue spec poking out of the sandy grains: a shard of turquoise blue sea glass – a rare find.

I picked the blue glass up and carefully placed it deep down in the pocket of my torn and ragged jeans. I pushed my hand down until I could feel the bottom of the pocket to ensure that there were no holes. I kept my hand around the glass for a few moments rubbing my fingers over its contours and against the ocean-smoothed edges. Turquoise blue I thought...what a find!

I gazed at my daughters frolicking and splashing in the waves, rolling their pant legs up higher and higher. We would begin our sea glass hunt within the hour; it was an annual ritual since the time the girls were babies strapped to my back. The sun was low on the horizon so it would be a short trek today. Tomorrow promised longer visits to some of the old haunts, including one we had named Sea Glass Beach.

Collecting sea glass has been part of my life for decades. The annual sea glass stroll with my young daughters on the beach holds many precious memories. Along the way, we have collected an assortment of worn shapes and sizes: brown, green, clear, and only occasionally, the treasured blue glass. Our standards were high and no jagged edges were allowed; we happily rejected sharp "newbies" and tossed them back into the sea for more churning. As the season moved forward, our finds were less frequent and our pockets less full.

Over the years our sea glass finds have diminished, and I remind myself and my girls that collecting sea glass was only part of our fun. The ocean breeze, surf, sea gulls, starfish, and endless slimy brown-green kelp lining the shore entwined with sea urchins and shells were part of the discovery and adventure too. Exploring the frothy blue beach landscape was fascinating as it stood in contrast to our life in the woods, lakes, and fields of the Green Mountains.

As my girls grew older, their enthrallment with collecting sea glass waned some but never completely faltered. They were content to let me walk the beach for hours while they spent time engaged in other activities, such as watching the surfers jumping the waves.

Sea glass continues to enchant me. Worn by rough seas, tossed over the waves until smooth and frosted, each brown, red, blue, or green gem began as castaway bottles and jagged broken glass. Then it is carried away by the currents, spun, churned, tumbled, and tossed with the tides. Sometimes it rests quietly on the ocean floor waiting for the tide to turn. Eventually it is tossed upon the rocks or cast upon the sandy shore, its ragged edges smoothed by time and tide and transformed into a treasure for beach collectors like me. Sometimes I sit quietly on the sand and contemplate the journey sea glass endures. Perhaps it offers a metaphor for life.

# More than Fish

The smell of the salty sea breeze is the first hint that we are almost at Weekapaug. We have passed Dunn's Corner, and even in the dark, our instinct is to roll down the car window. As we breathe in the air, I know that on the inland side the white heron are asleep in the marsh as are the fisherman and the sea creatures we will greet in the morning.

For twenty years we have been traveling to Weekapaug this same late October weekend for what we refer to as "the men's fishing weekend." But really, it is much more than that. For me, it is a time to enjoy the intense beauty of this area without the summer crowds, a time shared not with a spill of tourists but with local fishermen and women, as well as a few like-minded folks who meander down to enjoy the quiet season. For my two girls, Molly and Kate, it is the anticipation of our annual rituals on the salt-water pond and on the ocean beaches that spur their excitement.

Before sunup, our weekend fishermen rise with anticipation and eagerness. They are hoping for "stripers and blues" and the opportunity to be out in the waves without women and children. Each year has brought a range of catch, from an utter abundance to barren days without even a bite. When the men get out of the boat, their faces tell the story well before they utter a word. Despite days with limited edible results, they return with a bounty of stories told with enthusiasm and spirit, and it's clear to the women folk that catching fish is only part of their experience.

Each year, one of our favorite excursions is our trip to the salt-water pond for clamming. Clad with rubber boots, the kids and grown-ups pile into the back of a big pick-up truck for the bumpy journey to the far edge of the pond, which our host has assured us is the "best spot." It's low tide and expectant gulls fly overhead. In the distance, we spy a big heron jabbing its long beak in the sand to look for food. The clamming begins as everyone looks for "key holes" in the sand, which are the clams' long necks poking up toward the surface. Steamer clams are buried several inches down, and you don't have to dig deep to find them. We all take turns using the single clamming stick and between turns, we reach our bare hands into the cold sand hoping to find a clamshell. The bucket is filled quickly with so many helping hands.

As we dig, we find many more creatures that share this salt pond. The children are fascinated with the fiddler crab. During low tide, this small creature has burrowed into the mud near the high tidemark, making holes the size of a quarter. They come out only at low tide and otherwise return to their burrows. Occasionally we see a blue crab, recognizable by its blue, red, and olive colors, prowling along the bottom. We find minnows, several kinds of seaweed, horseshoe crab shells, and once we found a school of red jellyfish. There are various types of worms, many the size of a finger, which the children pull from the mud with excitement. When we return home, we often look these creatures up in books for identification. What I recall most however, is the kids' genuine fascination and excitement toward investigating all of the sea creatures that share this habitat, creatures not at home in the Green Mountains of Vermont.

Whether the sea is restless with frothy waves or calm, my girls and I also always go prospecting for another tiny sea treasure: worn colored glass washed ashore. I cherish these early morning and twilight strolls as together we poke underneath the shoreline rocks looking for soft worn shards of brown, green, and the more rare, turquoise and red glass.

By the time we are ready to leave the beach we will have scoured it several times finding a cornucopia of tiny treasures from the sea. We have the opportunity to really appreciate what lives on the shore and in the sea: stripers and blues, crabs and clams, starfish and jellyfish, driftwood, and salty pale glass. When we find sea creatures on shore, but still alive, we throw them back to sea with a superhero's smile and harbor the hope that we have spirited them to life once again.

The end of the day offers an opportunity to enjoy the day's catch – providing there is some! There are always steamers dipped in melted butter that are devoured quite quickly. And smoked bluefish paté is a definite favorite. We have prepared sea bass and bluefish in dozens of ways and have found that simply nothing compares to our fresh catch, no matter how well prepared.

Our annual late fall visits to Weekapaug offer our family a special connection to a wealth of natural treasures found in this flourishing habitat with its salt ponds, shoreline, and vast blue sea. It's so much more than fish.

# One Banana Split
# and Two Spoons

$\mathcal{I}$ often wonder if Roland found me, or if I found Roland. Some of the details of how and when we first became friends have dimmed in my memory. However, I do remember the evening when Roland and I first met. My mother and Roland lived in the same retirement community and were friends first. On one particular evening, my mother and I were en route to our own table for dinner when she stopped to greet Roland. He was clad in a blue-grey tweed jacket and had a twinkle in his eye. He was seated with a young man at a small dining table lit by a candle. We spoke only briefly as he was clearly enjoying the company of his handsome young grandson.

We began our friendship with non-stop luncheon conversations at the retirement community. We shared a mutual interest in environmental stewardship and a deep concern over global warming. Roland always had clippings in hand on environmental issues that he gave me to take home and read. He was a loyal follower of my monthly eco-focused column in our local newspaper, and when he couldn't locate it easily, he would telephone and ask me what page it was on.

One day, after several of these shared meals at his retirement community, Roland looked at me and said, "Next time, let's get out of this place!" So we began to have dinners out in restaurants and evenings together at the theater. Roland's stories fascinated me. Despite repeated recounts of his earlier years in England during World War II, I always wanted to hear them retold again. "Never give up," or "Fight till the bitter end," were expressions he'd recite in a bold and boisterous Winston Churchill voice. His words and manners endeared him to me and always made me smile.

One evening, I picked Roland up from the retirement community for a dinner out. I hoisted his wheelchair into the trunk and assisted him into the passenger seat of his silver Volvo sensing his excitement for an adventure away, even if it were only for a few hours. He was dressed in a kelly green blazer, black driving gloves, and beret. I asked him what he might like to do after dinner. It was a balmy evening with a light breeze and the sun was beginning to set. "Let's go for a drive," he said. So off we went, windows rolled down as we drove past cows and sheep grazing in fields with breathtaking lake vistas on the horizon. He was grinning throughout the entire drive. At one point, he reached over for my hand and called me by his deceased wife's name.

On another occasion, we had made plans to go to the theater and have dinner prior to the show at his favorite downtown eatery. I arrived to pick him up and found him quite excited. He clutched something in his hand and he said with a big smile, "I have a birthday coupon for tonight. We have a free dessert, and I get a free tee shirt." Later that evening as we dipped our two spoons into one very large banana split, I caught a glimpse of life as it comes in later years. The free tee shirt hung loosely on the empty chair next to me.

A few weeks later, I dropped my daughter off at her piano lesson, and my black Lab pup, Maggie, who was stuck waiting in the back seat, was itching for a walk. I decided to surprise

Roland and perhaps entice him outside with Maggie and me. It was a warm early fall evening with a lingering blue sky and setting sun. Roland was elated to see us and loved the idea of going outside. Before long we were traveling down the sidewalks with Maggie close at our side. Roland reached out and took her red leash. Maggie began to speed up and soon we were moving at a rapid speed, wheelchair and all careening around corners as I pleaded for Roland to drop the leash. But he was not letting go. The chair traveled faster and faster. Without many safer options at this point, I grabbed the wheelchair's handles and maneuvered us into a flowerbed of freshly planted white mums that then erupted into a thousand scattered white wisps. Dirt sprayed the sidewalk. But, we had stopped. When I turned from the disarray and looked at Roland, I saw him sitting with an enormous grin on his face. I burst out into laughter. Maggie wagged her tail happily. This hefty eighty-nine-year-old man with but one leg had had the time of his life racing in his small-scale chariot pulled on by a boisterous black dog.

Roland's friendship is a treasure for me. He's kind, caring, thoughtful, and fun. He is always ready with a story or a clipping to share. He always has a gleam in his eye and an eagerness to deliver his next Churchill quote of the day. I've hoisted his large-framed body into the front seat of his car finding reserves of strength I didn't know I had. We are friends. We are thirty-five years apart in age but close in heart and spirit. And we know how to share the delights of a crème brûlée or a banana split, served with two spoons.

# Lives Well Lived

When I reached fifty, I started noticing a few changes that were unexpected. People in my age group had begun to weave their health status into conversations: "I just had a colonoscopy"; "Have you had your bone density test yet?" Or, "How are your knees?" Conversations with my women friends centered on "the big M": the hot flashes and mood swings that are a part of menopause. People traded names of health practitioners like baseball cards. At times, it was almost comical, as I couldn't believe that this is what it would be like at middle age. More surprising was that I was attending more funerals than weddings – something I never believed could be true. That might not have been as hard to digest had it not been that the funerals were for people under fifty years old.

During the past sixteen months, three people in my life have died before turning fifty. One death was unexpected and the other two people had a terminal illness. I never really had a chance to say good-bye to any of them, but each person's death taught me more about living. Their death earlier than expected reminds me to embrace each day fully and with a spirit of gratitude.

Neil was killed in a car accident during the summer. He had been my younger daughter's reading tutor for a few years, but was more of a coach. She loved her sessions with Neil. He greeted her with bonjour every Tuesday at 5p.m., and she smiled knowing that he remembered that she had just come from French Club. He had an amazing gift with young people and inspired a love of learning through games and clever strategies, which engrossed the students fully and they weren't always aware that they were learning. He had a following, and I had been tenacious about getting him to be my daughter's tutor. Many had warned me of his popularity and that most of his students were young boys. However, I was unstoppable in my mission to secure Neil as Kate's tutor and succeeded. After only a few weeks with Neil, it was clear to me that he was a perfect fit for Kate. As the spring session ended, he went out and purchased two copies of the book *Where the Red Fern Grows,* one for Kate and one for me to read along with her during the summer months. Neil did these thoughtful things. Neil often had a beaded necklace around his neck or a bracelet, gifts given to him by his many student admirers. Accepting that Neil was dead at age thirty-eight was hard for our family and for the countless other families whose lives he had touched.

In the late fall of that same year, my neighbor John was diagnosed with Lou Gehrig's disease, also known as ALS. John was an active supporter of charities and a family man who loved his wife and children deeply. They were always together playing basketball and catch, or loading up the truck for weekends at their camp on the lake. He would snow blow our driveway during heavy snowstorms; I still owe him a batch of cookies for that kindness. As his ALS progressed, you saw less and less of him and more and more cars parked outside their home. John lost his mobility and his ability to talk.

One August afternoon as I finished packing the car for vacation, I was running late to get our dog Maggie to the kennel. I quickly backed my van out of our driveway and drove smack into the door of a shiny new Chevy Impala. I heard a loud crunch and my daughters' two voices from the back seat bellowing "Mom!" I knocked sheepishly on John's back door and explained the unfortunate accident to a pleasant redheaded gentleman, John's brother-in-law, who calmly listened to my story. He told me that he understood, and he didn't even seem very upset. He told me to go on vacation and we'd deal with the issue in a week. We exchanged the necessary information and I drove away slowly. A smashed car door seemed trivial to him when compared to sitting bedside with his brother-in-law who was unable to speak.

John got quite a charge out of the story, as he had been privy to previous tales of my driving that had also resulted in dents and broken car parts.

Months later, toward the final weeks of his life, I visited John at the respite house. I retold the story and managed to get a big smile from him. Later his wife shared with me that the day I visited was one of his better days, and she asked me what I had talked about because she had heard that he had a big smile on his face. I told her that it was the Chevy Impala story. At John's memorial service, the car story came up many times. It seems as though John liked it so much that friends and family joked about it repeatedly. I realized then that perhaps I was meant to plow into the car that day as it had given my dying friend cause to smile more than once during his final weeks.

The following summer, I received word that my cousin Andrew had succumbed to a brain tumor, a condition that he had been coping with for more than fifteen years. When we learned of his failing health, my brother and I had planned to visit him in Baltimore but were waiting until the end of baseball season. We waited too long; I never was able to say goodbye to one of my favorite cousins. It took me a while to get over my guilt. Like John, Andrew was only forty-eight when he died and left a loving wife and family behind too.

We attended the simple graveside service for Andrew at Lake George. I saw cousins whom I had not seen since their weddings, many of which took place seventeen years ago. None of us could believe that so much time had passed. Now the old saying that we only see loved ones at weddings and funerals felt poignant and true.

After the service, I stood by a wooden box on a small table placed in front of a birch tree that held my cousin's ashes. I spoke to him wishing that it could have been in person, and I made a promise to stay in closer touch with the extended family we shared. Back at the reception held at cousin Randy's house, we all sat around telling story after story about Andrew and my father, who was their uncle Hank. Tears and laughter filled the room and the hours moved forward. We all enjoyed being together again. They told us that Andrew had put together a video of his life in the final weeks, something for his thirteen-year-old son and his wife to have as a remembrance. When it came time for the accompanying music, Andrew had insisted on playing a song by the Doors, "This is the End." Despite a unanimous plea for any soundtrack but that, Andrew was tenacious in his choice. He felt grateful for the sixteen years he had been given to live after his diagnosis, and he understood that this was now his life's end. I watched the video with tears streaming down my face and saw many touching images of my cousin: standing by his bride at their wedding, building architectural models, sitting in a wheelchair, deep sea fishing, as well as eating crème-filled donuts. He had lived his life fully and with a positive spirit. He had made peace with his mortality and he was prepared to say good-bye. Andrew's song choice epitomized his full acceptance of life from beginning to end.

Three vibrant lives. Taken by surprise. What is the deeper message when they leave and are so relatively young...what can we learn? Perhaps, their dying reminds us to live; perhaps it causes us to pause... and think.

# Birthing a Book

*I*n my mid twenties, a college friend offered me a job as an assistant innkeeper at a Vermont country inn located in a small town near Middlebury. The current innkeepers needed help and I jumped at the opportunity, as I had always dreamed of running a country inn. It was an idyllic setting with colorful flowerbeds, an herb garden, and pigs and goats in the pasture. We baked fresh bread every day and prepared gourmet meals for interesting guests that hailed from all over the country. We served tea and homemade chocolate chip cookies. We made beds, cleaned rooms, and regularly chased the pigs that were often let loose by the goats. That is another story.

It wasn't long before I realized that this 5a.m. to 10p.m. seven days a week job was far from my original idyllic vision. It was by far the hardest job I have ever had, and after nine months, I was ready to bid it farewell. I listed it on my resume and spoke of the experience often. In doing so, I discovered that there are throngs of people who share the same idyllic vision of running a county inn. It seemed to help me during the job interview process too, as almost every prospective employer asked me what it was like to run a country inn after seeing it on my resume.

During my mid thirties, I brought that same idyllic vision to the birth of my first daughter. I made the decision early on that I was going to go the natural childbirth route and manage my pain just with breathing, breathing, and more breathing: absolutely no drugs. I remember friends and family repeatedly trying to convince me otherwise, explaining that it would be much more comfortable if I considered having an epidural. Stubbornly, I held my ground. Later, I found myself three weeks overdue and after many thwarted attempts to encourage the baby's delivery, I had an emergency c-section complete with drugs. My idealistic vision of childbirth was derailed.

Nonetheless, I am still an idealist, and when I agreed to write my very first book of short stories I let that same idealism take hold.

Writing a book is reminiscent of birthing a child. It begins as this amazing romantic vision and then it involves a lot of hard work. You move through so many different emotions, thoughts, and revisions. There are days when you are excited to share your thoughts with the world and other days when you are terrified. You remind yourself that you have taken countless writing classes and seminars; you have participated in writing groups and have written a monthly column for several years. You have been a book-reading groupie where you listen to authors read from their books as you calmly sip wine and eat cheese.

As you move through the process, you build up your confidence only to have it deflate whenever you step into a bookstore and see countless other authors' books packed on the shelves with colorful covers and interesting titles. You imagine that lucky day when your book will sit on a shelf in a store and then you worry that nobody will buy your book, or far worse, that people will buy your book but won't like it. It's an emotional rollercoaster.

I worked diligently to write while fitting it into my busy life as a working mom. Thankfully, my friends were supportive, and particularly, my close friend Jennifer was a huge help with several of the stories where there were struggles; her style and playfulness with words were a blessing.

The day before my stories were due to the editor, my friend Philip Baruth, who was running for political office, telephoned me to ask if I would write a letter to the editor to support his election to the state senate. I believed in Philip and told him I would do anything I could to help him win the election. After writing this letter, I found that my entire body was shaking when I pushed the submit and send button. I had just written my personal thoughts for many people to read in the news. However, in retrospect, this was a gift from Philip because it pushed me to step forward and in turn, this helped me to brave moving forward with the book. Writing and publishing this book has required courage, humility, and another leap of faith. Now once again I hope that I can land on my feet.

Throughout my life, I have been a risk taker and I have learned much from these risks, failures, and successes. Ultimately, if one or two of the stories in this collection touches people's lives, I will be happy. Better yet, if I inspire others to write, tell, and share their stories too, I will be even happier. We all have good stories to share.

"The purpose of life is to live it, to taste experience to the utmost, to reach out eagerly and without fear for newer and richer experience."

—*Eleanor Roosevelt*

## About the Artists

The late Dr. James Madison, a close family friend of the Caswells, painted the original watercolor image of Humpty reproduced on the book cover.

Annie Caswell, Laurie Caswell Burke's sister, did all of the black and white line drawings in the book. Annie has been a freelance artist since 1981. She has exhibited her work in the United States, Europe, and the U.S. Virgin Islands. Images of her paintings, sculpture, and spirit dolls can be found on her website  www.anniecaswell.com and are available for purchase through her business, "Kissed by Fire."